A BEGINNER'S GUIDE
TO
STARTING AND GROWING
A
YOUTUBE CHANNEL

What to Expect

The goal of this book is to provide all the information that you may/will need to start a YouTube channel. This book will take you on a journey where you will learn about setting up your own channel, lighting, editing and uploading videos. The last chapter of this book will give some very important tips that will help you to increase number of subscribers of your channel.

What makes this book unique is that in this book we will talk about everything that is involved in setting up a channel. Whether its lighting (3-point), camera, tripod, umbrella, editing, uploading or marketing.

Who should buy this book:

a) If you are interested in knowing, what it takes to start your own YouTube channel.
b) You want to understand the basics of a Camera.
c) You want to learn how to set up lighting, increase subscribers and view count.
d) Free Support: You can email me at cloudsimplifiedforyou@gmail.com for any questions (technical or related to book) you may have. Typically, I will answer your question in 1-2 business days. Please limit your questions to topics discussed in this book. Thank you, kindly.

Table of Contents

Chapter One – Getting Started

Whether you are looking to convert your passion into a business, or you want to do it as a hobby, YouTube provides a great platform. With over a Billion active users, opportunities are endless. In developing countries, such as India, it is estimated that there are 225 million users on mobile alone. This number is expected to reach 400 million users in the next couple of years. What that means is new users are joining every day. If you set up your channel right, post regularly, you can capture these users and grow your subscriber base. More subscribers you have; more will be the view count of videos you post and that could potentially mean more money in your pocket.

The goal of this book is to provide you all the information that you need to start and grow your channel. First, we will look at how to create a new YouTube channel, and then we will talk about basics of camera and learn some video editing techniques that will help you in creating high quality videos. In the end, we will talk about some different strategies that we can implement to increase subscribers.

Why YouTube:

YouTube is not only the 2nd largest search engine, it gets second largest amount of traffic as well. Whether we are looking for a recipe, a solution to a problem, sports or any other topic, YouTube is quite often the place where we go. Unlike some other platforms, YouTube reaches across ages, cultures and demographics. You can pick any audience you like, and it has a large enough presence in YouTube.

YouTube SEO:

You do not need an account to watch videos on YouTube. You can simply go to YouTube.com, type your search criteria and search for videos. YouTube will display list of videos, based on your search criteria and you can click on them and watch.

However, if you want more personalized experience, then you can create a new YouTube account or log in with existing account. This way YouTube can learn your "preferences", type of videos you watch and can recommend similar videos next time you log in. You can also create a playlist and add your favorite videos to it. Next time when you log in, you can directly go to your playlist and watch your favorite videos.

When a user on YouTube performs a search for some content, YouTube uses algorithm to search for related videos and then ranks these videos based on what search engine considers more relevant. The algorithm primarily uses parameters like watch time, session time to rank videos. SEO or Search Engine Optimization is a technique that can be used so that your videos rank above other videos. The higher the ranking your video gets, more likely user will see your video. We will discuss about SEO later in this book.

How YouTubers Make Money:

You might have noticed that most YouTube videos start with an Advertisement, which is how YouTubers make money. This is called monetization. YouTube has certain rules around that and you must meet certain criteria's before you can start placing advertisements on your videos. We will talk about them in Chapter 4.

What is a YouTube Channel:

A YouTube Personal Channel is a User's Profile page. It consists of your name, nature of your account, your videos. You can also customize the background and color scheme of your channel. Businesses can have their channels as well. These channels are different from personal channels because they can have more than one owner.

How to Create a YouTube Channel:

Now that we have covered the basics, it is time for some action. Let us see how to create a new YouTube Channel. First, login into YouTube using your google account. Click on the gear icon to get into your account's YouTube Settings (See snapshot below).

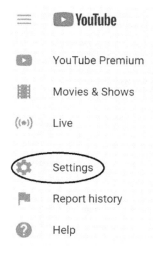

Under Account Settings, you will see different options and links. Click on "Create a new channel" link.

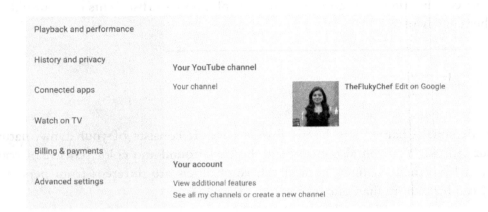

After you click on the "Create a new channel" link, you will be asked to choose your brand account name. It is very important to choose the right name. Think about what type of content you will be posting, your targeted audience. Come up with 5-6 different names and choose what you think is best for your channel. Click on "Create" button to create your channel.

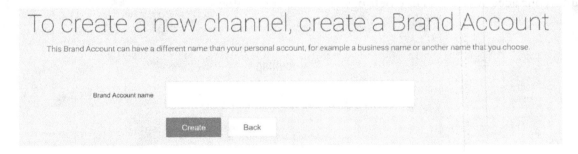

Chapter Two – Equipment

After your channel is set up, you would need some basic equipment before you can start shooting videos. Let us look at them:

Camera:

You can film your videos using iPhone or other smart phones. If you want better quality, you can buy one of the DSLR cameras. It really comes down to your budget and the quality of videos you desire. Some people start with iPhone and slowly move towards a professional camera as their subscribers base grow.

If you are going to shoot using a professional camera, you have two options. One is to let camera decide on settings (Automatic mode) or the other one is to you can be in control of all settings (Manual mode). I strongly recommend you to be in charge and use Manual Mode. In order to do so, it is essential to understand the following three camera settings.

a) Shutter Speed : Shutter speed is the length of time a camera shutter is open to expose light into the camera sensor. It is typically measured in fractions of a second. Slow shutter speeds mean more light into camera sensor. If you are shooting in dark or low light, you should use slow shutter speed. If you are shooting in natural light, you can use fast shutter speed.

b) Aperture: A hole within a lens, through which light travels into the camera body. The larger the hole, more light can pass in and reach camera sensor. Think of it like a window in your house. Bigger the window, more light can come in your house. Aperture also controls area of image that will appear sharp. Aperture is typically measured in "f" numbers (f/1.4, f/2.0, f/4.0 etc). F/1.4 means bigger hole, more light and background will appear blurry. F/4.0 means smaller hole as compared to F/1.4, which leads to less light and background will be less blurry. If you are shooting a portrait then you want your background to be blurry so that whoever watches your video/picture only looks at the object on focus, without getting distracted about items in the background.

c) ISO –ISO refers to the light sensitivity. It is typically measured in numbers. Larger the number, brighter your video will be. However, if you increase it too much, it adds noise to the image. Examples of ISO: 100, 200, 400, 800, 1600. Typically, you will use ISO of 200 or 400.

Controlling the light is important because shooting with too much light and you will have an over-exposed image, and not enough light gives you an under-exposed image. Using right combination of shutter speed, Aperture and ISO, you can control the light.

Let us look at an example:

| Underexposed | Overexposed | Correct Exposure |

All the images shown above were taken at same time of the day, under same light conditions but different camera settings. On the left side, is an underexposed image. As you can see image is very dark and shows very little detail. In the middle is an overexposed image. The image is brighter than it should be, and is not pleasant to the eyes. The best way to learn about these settings is to take an object, and take bunch of pictures with different combinations of ISO, Aperture and Shutter speed.

Zebra Pattern:

To help you set the exposure correctly, most cameras come with Zebra settings. Zebras are black and white striped patterns. They are there to show areas that are overexposed or close to overexposed. You need to turn "ON" Zebra settings on your camera to see these patterns. If you see lot of zebra pattern while taking a picture or shooting a video, you can adjust the exposure to reduce or eliminate zebra pattern.

Lens:

Before buying a lens, you will need to know the sensor size of your camera. It will probably be one of these

- Full-frame
- APS-C
- Micro Four Thirds

Full Frame cameras are typically very expensive. They are the best in terms of image quality. Most DSLRs will have APS-C sensor. Micro Four Thirds are smallest of these and are becoming increasingly popular. A lens with 50 mm focal length will look more zoomed in when used on a "Micro Four Thirds" camera than on an APS-C. Let us look at some basics of lens.

a) **Focal Length**: Focal length is usually measured in millimeters. It tells us the angle of view and the magnification. The longer the focal length, the narrower the angle of view and the higher the magnification. Therefore, if you are taking a picture from a good distance and you see that it is zoomed a lot when you open this picture in computer, then you are probably using a longer focal length. Depending on your channel, you will have to choose what lens will work best for you. Example, if you are starting a beauty channel you would want a lens with high focal length. On the other hand, if you are shooting outside, say in mountains and you want to show more area around you, you would go with a lens with smaller focal length.

b) **Zoom or Prime Lens**: Prime lenses have a fixed focal length. On the other hand, zoom lenses have variable focal lengths. The advantage of zoom lens that you can use it for different purpose. If you want a wide-angle view, you can reduce the focal length, if you want a zoomed view you can increase it.
Prime lenses are smaller in size and weight. In general, Prime lens have better image quality than Zoom lens.

Tripod:

You can take pictures or shoot video by holding the camera in hand but you will most likely have a camera shake. That's where Tripod can help. You can mount camera on a tripod and press record button to records videos or take a picture. You do not have to worry about shaking. If you need more flexibility, you can also buy a Head and attach it to a tripod. The advantage of using head is that you can move camera up and down without touching the camera. This is helpful if you want to shoot top down videos. Below is a picture of tripod with head for your reference.

If you are interested in buying above product here is a link to it: https://amzn.to/2wrNDmy

Lighting:

As a beginner starting out, you would think that investing in a good camera or lens is enough. However, you will be surprise to hear that without good lighting, this investment might not give you desired results. Depending on the type of channel you are starting, you can buy your lighting sets. If it is a beauty channel, you can buy a Ring light; if you are shooting in the kitchen, you can replace the ceiling yellow lights with white lights. No matter what type of channel it is, if you understand the concept of 3-point lighting, you can illuminate the subject properly and control the amount of shadows. As the name suggest, you need 3 lights to use this technique.

TIP: Just remember; when you buy lights make sure they come with an adjustable stand. Quite often, you will have to move your lights up and down to illuminate the subject.

The Key Light

The primary light is the key light. It is there to bring light directly to your subject so that whatever you are filming, the subject is well illuminated in the shot. You can place Key light behind your camera or at 45 degrees to your camera. This light, most likely will have more than one bulb, in other words it should give maximum light as compared to other lights.

Example of a key light: Fovitec Softbox Lighting Kit (See snapshot below)

Amazon Website link for this product: https://amzn.to/2LwhyzI

The Fill Light

The fill light fills the dark side of your subject. It is on opposite side of key light. If you use only key light, one side of the subject will be dark.

The Back Light

As the name suggests, back light is used to illuminate the area behind the subject. This will help in reducing any shadows that may fall on the wall directly behind subject.

Here is a typical set up for 3-point lighting.

Standard Three-Point Lighting

#3 Back Light

#1 Key Light

Object

#2 Fill Light

Note: This picture has been taken from Wikipedia.

You do not have to go by the books; you can set up lights however you want. Here is an example of how I used the 3-point lighting for shooting one of the videos for my client.

Silver Photo Studio Reflector Umbrella

To distribute light evenly and eliminate glare and spots, you should put either reflective or shoot through umbrella in front of lights.

Here is a picture showing light with reflective umbrella.

Amazon Website link for this product: https://amzn.to/2MV39la

White Balance Gray Reference Reflector Grey Card

If you are shooting in conditions where levels of light are changing quite often, it is always good to do a custom white balance in camera. This will assure that objects that appear white in person are rendered white. Just snap a picture holding white balance cards and choose to set your white balance in camera or during post processing. Here is a picture to show you how this card looks. You can buy it on Amazon or any other website.

Amazon Website link for this product: https://amzn.to/2obk2Ki

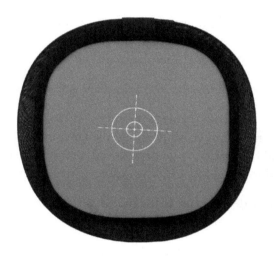

Chapter Three —Editing and Uploading Videos

Editing Videos:

After you are done shooting your video, you will have to use a video editing software to edit the videos. Editing may involve trimming the clip, adding voice, music, or text to your videos. Most of the time when you shoot a video, you will not shoot all at once. You may have more than one clip and you will have to combine these clips to make your final video.

There are lot of software's available online for editing but the one I highly recommend is "Adobe Premiere Elements 2018". It runs for about $107 including taxes. The reason I am recommending it is because it is very easy to learn. If you have "Pluralsight" membership, you can watch videos by "Kelsey Brannan". Her course "Premiere Elements Fundamentals" is absolutely amazing and covers everything you need to know to start editing videos using "Adobe Premiere Elements 2018". This course is free, if you have "Pluralsight" membership.

Normally editing your videos will involve the following steps

1) Transferring your videos from camera memory card to an external Hard Dive. I strongly recommend using an external hard drive. Editing a software takes a lot of memory, so it is better to store them on an external hard drive. Needless to say, that it will serve as a backup in the event your experience a technical failure or glitch with the software or laptop.

2) Importing videos using video editing software. This step is basically telling software that these are the videos I want to use for my project.

3) Dragging videos to "Timeline" on your video editing software. Most video editors will have a Timeline, on which you can drag your videos. You will drag the in the order you want to see them in the final video. After you drag videos, you can edit them.

Note: Even if you drag them in wrong order, you do not have to worry. You can still move the around in the time line by dragging them.

4) Trimming, applying transitions and effects (for color, lighting, crop). This step is most time consuming. You need to pick best parts from each clip and then combine them into one. Since these clips may be shot at different times, locations or angles, it is possible that when you combine them, there is a sudden change of position or surroundings. If that's the case, then you can put a transition between the clips. A Transition can convey passage of time, change of location. You also want to make sure that lighting is consistent across your clips. If that's not the case then you can apply lighting effects to increase or decrease light in the video.

5) Adding music to your video (optional). If there are certain parts in video where you are not doing talking, then I highly recommend putting some music there so that audience does not get bored and leave. There are some websites that allow you to download Royalty Free Music and add it to your video. One website which I really like and recommend is "https://www.bensound.com/". Feel free to check it out and download some music for your video.

You will have to watch, edit and repeat the cycle multiple times, before you can finalize your video.

Uploading Videos:

Alright, so the hard work is done and finally it's time to upload your video. Depending on size of your video and your internet speed, it may take several hours to upload video on YouTube. The best approach here is to start uploading your video as soon as you are done with editing a video.

To upload a Video, click on "+" sign and then click on Upload video.

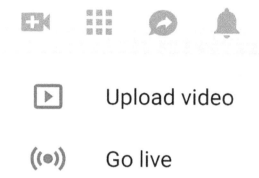

You will be presented with the following screen. Make sure to select "Private" from the dropdown (see snapshot below). After upload is complete, you want to make sure video looks good before you make it public and your subscribers are notified. You can select your video file and upload it.

As your video is uploading, you can utilize this time to think about what you might want to put in the description box, tags and other fields. Before we look into that further, let's learn some search optimization techniques.

Search Engine Optimization:

As mentioned earlier, YouTube uses an algorithm to bring back the results in an order when a user does a search on YouTube. This algorithm focuses on how audience interacts with videos. Let us say you posted a video, which is 3-minute long. YouTube will keep track on how long users are watching your video – which is called watch time or view time. For example, if your viewers watched on an average for say 15 seconds, YouTube will rank your video lower. The algorithm will think that users are not finding your video interesting. That's why it is very important to include information (content) that is useful to the viewers to keep them engaged and interested until the end. Other quantizable markers such as number of likes, dislikes and comments also contribute to how your video will be ranked.

Before we worry about watch time, we need to make sure users can find our video. To achieve that, we need to optimize our video metadata (Titles, description, Tags) so that search engine can rank us higher.

Here are the things you can do to optimize videos:

1) Think carefully about what title you want to give to your video: The title is the first thing people will read when scrolling through a list of videos, so make sure it's clear and compelling. Keep title to about 60 character and try to include important keywords in beginning of title. You can also do some keyword search to see what users are searching for and include that in your title. Here is a link that google provides where you can see what words are being searched by users.

   Link: https://trends.google.com/trends/

2) Prepare description of your video. Every video you upload, you can put description about video in the "description" section. Use this as an opportunity to describe purpose of your video, any tips you may have that are not part of video or any other details you want your users to know.

3) List of Tags: You can highlight main keywords in your tags. You must think carefully of what you want in your tags. Tags plays a very important role in ranking your video. Tag your important keywords first.

   TIP: you can list popular channels related to your video in tags. This way when someone is watching their video, your video will appear on the side list as well.

4) Custom Thumbnail: Your video thumbnail will be the main image viewers will see when scrolling through a list of video results, and it can have a large impact on the number of views you will get. YouTube will auto-generate a few thumbnail options for your video, but It is highly recommend uploading a custom thumbnail. YouTube reports that "90% of the best performing videos on YouTube have custom thumbnails. The recommended custom thumbnail size by YouTube is **1280*720px**. However, if you wish, you could use up to **1920*1080**. Image formats could be .JPG, .GIF, .BMP, or .PNG. There is an image size limit to keep in mind- 2MB. If you take an image using 4k camera or DSLR, your image size could be 7MB or more. You may have to resize the photos. However, if you take using an iPhone, your image size will be around 2MB and it will work out great.

TubeBuddy:

If SEO seems too much work and you are willing to spend few bucks per month, then there are some software's available that can help you to achieve search optimization. One of them, which I highly recommend is "TubeBuddy". You can buy its subscription for about 5 dollars per month.

TubeBuddy is a browser extension built for YouTube creators that can save hours of time, help optimize videos. Let us see how we can use TubeBuddy to do search optimization.

1) After you have added "TubeBuddy" extension to your browser. Go to Youtube.com and search for some content. For our example, we will search for "how to grow YouTube channel". See the results below.

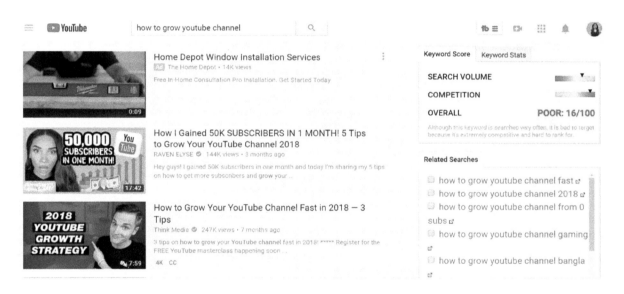

As you can see from above snapshot, TubeBuddy has given an overall score of 16 to this search keyword. What it means is TubeBuddy recommend us not to use "how to grow YouTube channel" as tag in our video. Not only it tells us that, it also recommends us tags that we can use for our video.

2) Now click on "Tb" link and then click on Tag Explorer.

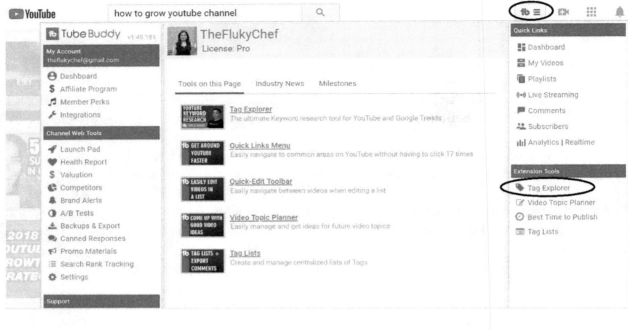

It will open a window like below.

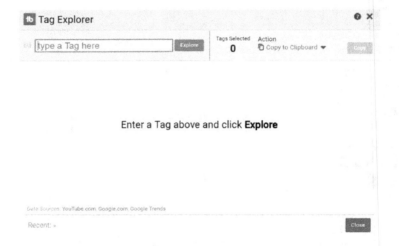

Type in the same text "how to grow YouTube channel" and click on explore button. Then go to "Auto-Suggested" Tab. See snapshot below.

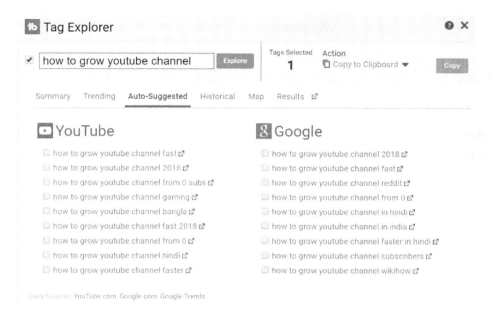

As you can see, there are two list above. One is for YouTube and other is for Google. These lists contain what Google or YouTube will suggest as user types in. Therefore, using these tags will increase chances that more users will see your video. These are just some of the features that "TubeBuddy" offers. You can learn more about TubeBuddy on https://www.tubebuddy.com/

After you have set up all the information for the video, it's finally time to make it public. As soon as you make it public, your subscribers will get an email or YouTube notification, alerting them about your newest upload.

NOTE: Before making it public, add end Cards and End Screens to your video. Read next chapter for more details about it.

Recently, YouTube changed its policy for monetization. As per the new policy the eligibility requirement for monetization is 4,000 hours of watch time within the past 12 months and 1,000 subscribers. What this means for you is that before you can start making any money, you must have more than thousand subscribers and more than four thousand hours of watch time. Though this policy is not good for small channels, it was very much needed so that YouTube can control fake videos, Bot subscribers. You will be surprised to know that you can buy "Views" or "subscribers". There are so many websites that let you do that.

Let's see how we can increase number of views/Subscribers.

1) **Know your Target Audience**: Once you have figured out what kind of channel you are starting, you need to think about your target audience. For example: Let us say you are starting a cooking channel. You decided to make a black bean salad. Now if you are targeting audience in US that works fine, but If you are targeting audience in India, it won't work out that well. Black Beans are available in very few cities in India. Therefore, it is very important to know your target audience. You can plan you content accordingly. You should try to keep your content engaging and interesting. The more people can relate to it, more likely they will watch your video until end and possibly watch your other videos too.

2) **Post Regularly**: It is very important to be consistent with your uploads. Unless you video goes viral, it may take 6-12 months of continuous uploads to build up user base. Initially you may feel like your content is not perfect, or video quality is not at its best but do not worry about it and keep posting. If you post regularly, you will build up solid content on your channel and your video will start showing up in search results more often. Once a user visit your channel and see that you upload continuously, they are more likely to subscribe to your channel.

3) **Keep on Improving**: Initially it is important to take feedback from your friends, relatives. See what they feel about your videos and what areas you can improve. Ask them to give you honest opinion with constructive feedback.

Maybe you start shooting videos with an iPhone initially, but as your user base grows you can upgrade to some professional equipment, lighting. Most YouTubers use DSLRs along with accessories like Tripods, lenses, Microphone. Remember, though, that a good camera is not everything. If you neglect other things like audio quality and lighting, your viewers may still lose interest in your videos after first few seconds and won't subscribe to you at all.

Keep on finding ways to improve your content, surprise your viewers. Be selective with clips you include in your final cut.

4) **Connect with your Viewers**: One way to connect with viewers is by posting interesting, useful and high-quality content. However, that's not enough. You should try to engage as much as possible with your viewers. Whether it's replying to their comments, taking videos request from them. Viewers should feel they relate to you and it is not just like thousands of other channels.

5) **Add Cards and End Screens to your Video**: After you upload your videos to YouTube, you can still edit them using YouTube editor. This is useful in case you miss something small and you do not want to spend hours in uploading video again. Apart from editing, you can add End Screens or Cards in your videos to poll viewers, link to external sites, or direct people to other videos.

To add Cards or End Screens, click on "Creator Studio".

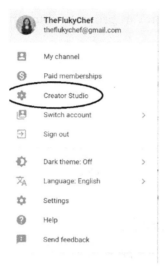

After you do that, you will list of all your videos. Then click on "Edit" in front of the video in which you want to add end screen.

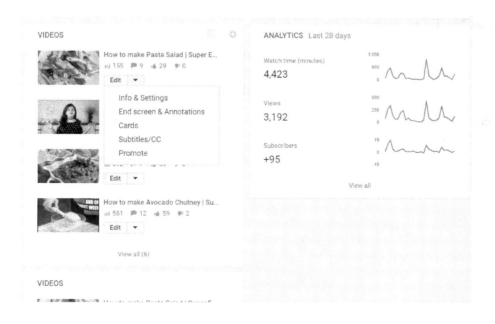

Cards are small notifications that appear in the top, right-hand corner of both desktop and mobile screens. You can include up to five cards per video, but if you are including multiple cards, be sure to space them out evenly to give viewers time to take the desired action.

End Screens are rectangular notifications that appear in the left side of your video (see snapshot below). To add an End Screen in your video, click on edit video and then click on "End Screen & Annotations". Then click on "Add element" (see snapshot below). You can add a video from your collection, a "Subscribe Button" or you can promote your other channel. After you add it, click on "Save Button" to save your changes.

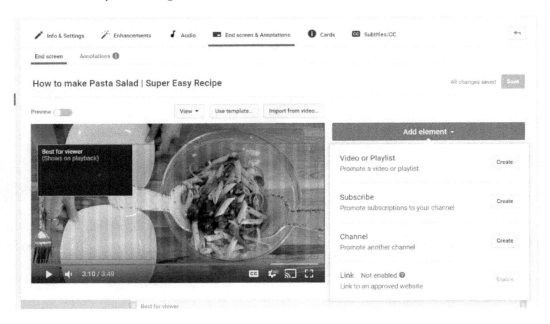

6) Use Social Media to generate cross Traffic:

Post Link to your videos on Facebook, pictures on Instagram. Ask your family members and friends to like, subscribe and share it with their friends. Your goal should be to bring users to your YouTube channel from different platforms. YouTube is all about connecting and sharing with other users.

If you are curious and you want to see where all your views are coming from then you can do that easily. YouTube provides "Analytics". Click on "Creator Studio" link. Then click on "Analytics" followed by traffic sources to see where your views are coming from (see snapshot below)

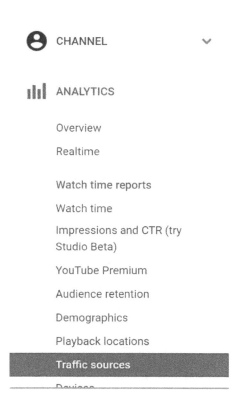

Traffic source	Watch time (minutes) ↓	Views	Average view duration	Average percentage viewed
External	387 (32%)	186 (28%)	2:04	45%
YouTube search	229 (19%)	137 (21%)	1:40	49%
Channel pages	220 (18%)	133 (20%)	1:39	39%
Browse features	108 (9.0%)	58 (8.8%)	1:51	42%
Suggested videos	99 (8.3%)	50 (7.6%)	1:59	46%
Other YouTube features	85 (7.1%)	55 (8.3%)	1:32	36%
Notifications	52 (4.3%)	29 (4.4%)	1:47	40%
Direct or unknown	12 (1.0%)	7 (1.1%)	1:46	42%
Playlist page	5 (0.4%)	3 (0.5%)	1:33	40%

You can also look at country from which you are getting most views. To do so, you can click on "Demographics" and then click on Geography (see snapshot below). It is very important to keep track of these parameters. Once you know what group of people are most interested in your videos, you can change your content and start targeting these users.

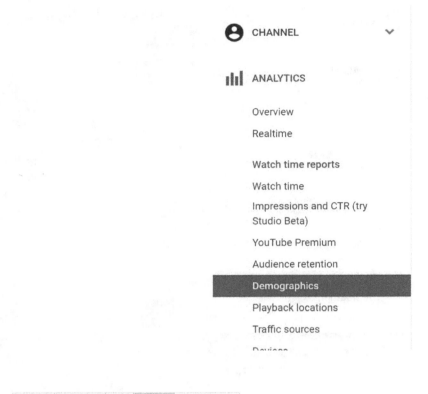

Geography	Watch time (minutes) ⓘ ↓	Male	Female
India	1,027 (25%)	24%	76%
United States	387 (9.2%)	100%	0.0%
Unknown region ⓘ	178 (4.2%)	100%	0.0%
			1-3 of 3

In the end, I just want to wish you good luck for your channel. I sincerely hope that this book provided you all the information you were looking for.

THANK YOU

That's all I wanted to cover in this book. Thank you for reading my book. If you have any questions or suggestions related to book, feel free to email me at cloudsimplifiedforyou@gmail.com.